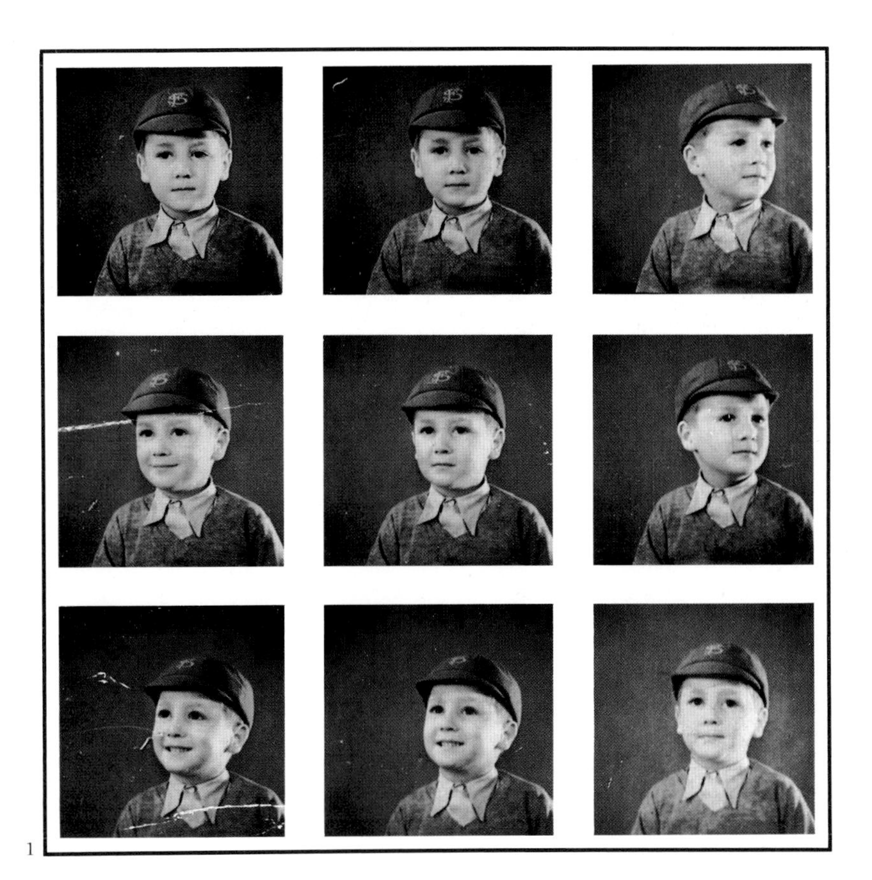

1

The Faces of JOHN LENNON

DEZO HOFFMANN

Written by Norman Jopling

McGraw-Hill Book Company

New York St. Louis San Francisco Hamburg Mexico Toronto

Other books by Dezo Hoffmann
The Beatle Book
With the Beatles
The Rolling Stones
The Beatles Conquer America

First published in the United States of America and Canada in 1986
by McGraw-Hill Book Company

1 2 3 4 5 6 7 8 9 8 7 6

ISBN 0-07-029306-6

INTRODUCTION

Far from fading into the receding glow of the 'sixties, the Beatles are now established as part of popular mythology. It fell to Dezo Hoffmann, whose wartime cinematographic adventures later turned gracefully to the more leisurely pastimes of showbusiness, to chronicle visually their rise to fame. Particularly precious are his memories and images of John Lennon.

These, many of them previously unpublished, are now presented for the first time as a collection.

Here, then, is John, his fascination undimmed, whose achievements touched us all, seen from the days when the Beatles were unheard of outside Liverpool, up until and through the phenomenal years of international Beatlemania. The images speak for themselves, but here also are Dezo's own comments on his work with the Beatles and especially his affectionate yet fractious relationship with John.

'I first met the Beatles in 1962 when I was a freelance photographer specializing in showbusiness. I was contributing pictures to the international press, such as *Cash Box* and *Billboard*, to Fleet Street dailies such as the *Daily Mirror* and *The News Chronicle*, and at the other end of the scale I was staff photographer for a small London pop-music weekly called *Record Mirror*.

'One day, at the regular *Record Mirror* weekly editorial meeting, there were the usual piles of readers' letters to look through. Something attracted me to a pink, very nicely scented letter, and as I picked it up out fell a snapshot. It was a colleague who noticed the picture, and as he handed it to me I was intrigued without even reading the letter. The photograph was of four guys with long hair – unusual to see in those days. I read the letter and the girl was sobbing her heart out; you could imagine the teardrops on the letter. In fact she was complaining that we never wrote about this group called the Beatles, who had just returned from Hamburg to Liverpool, and already had a record out in Germany on Polydor. I was fascinated by the sentiment of the letter and I suddenly realized that this was quite a good human-interest story.

'I spoke to the editor, Jimmy Watson, and suggested we did a feature on these Beatles, but he laughed, saying we couldn't take every reader's letter to heart. Luckily, I had strong support from Roy Burden, our circulation manager, who saw the advantages of featuring a Liverpool group, because at that time *Record Mirror* did not sell well outside London. It took us a good six months of bombarding Jimmy Watson to arrange a trip to Liverpool and also to locate the Beatles, but to this day I'm still grateful to Jimmy, because he finally succumbed to my idea.

'Eventually I met them in the NEMS office in Liverpool, and Brian Epstein was there to welcome us. The boys hadn't arrived, but I'll never forget them trooping in one by one, their hair neat and tidy, wearing beautiful ties and new suits, all ready for their first national press interview. My feeling was that Epstein wanted to impress the boys with his London contacts, and he wanted me to take pictures of them all signing contracts. But I didn't want "signing" pictures; I told them I hadn't come all the way from London to take a picture which could have been taken in London or anywhere else. I explained that everybody has those stereotyped pictures; they're all the same, only the faces change. I wanted pictures with a local flavour. And as I said those things, I could feel the whole atmosphere of the room change. With that, it was just as if I'd bought myself a bunch of four boys – saying I didn't want to photograph them in the office. They didn't want to be photographed in the office either.

'As my first impressions of them were of four clean-cut boys, this was the way I wanted to portray them. I didn't want to photograph them in the drab streets of Liverpool, or put them in a crane or a dock. I didn't want them to look dirty, I wanted to emphasize the boys, not Liverpool.

'The first series of pictures we took were at Paul's house with John and Paul making tea, the boys messing around in the garden and around the house. Then the idea came to me to somehow portray the vivacity, the life in them. You could portray that every second of their lives, because they really loved . . . to live. So I thought to myself – jumping! But there was nowhere to jump, and on top of that they were already very popular in Liverpool, so there would be problems with fans.

'I said, "Can we go somewhere you could make a jump? It will be quite a simple thing, but there must be a little hill and I will be underneath the hill so that when you jump, you don't have to jump a lot. I would lie on the grass, shooting upwards."

'They didn't quite understand what I wanted, and that was mainly because of my foreign accent. At that time it was really thick, thicker than their Liverpool accent, and this is when Paul began to be my tutor in English, which is rather funny – a Liverpudlian teaching a Hungarian English. My main problem was with the letter "W".

'The boys suggested we go to Sefton Park, and so we set off in Paul's car. There we found a sort of a hill which sloped very slightly downwards. Anyway, I found one spot where I could visualize the picture and I wanted them to jump in unison. I had only half a film in the camera before I re-wound, and I said to myself, "Only six exposures left . . . will they be able to jump together?" But really it turned out to be very easy, mainly because of the boys' natural intelligence. They knew exactly what to do, and anyway, they were jumping beans all the time. You can see from the photograph how well they jumped together. I told them to be careful not to hide each other's faces with their arms and hands, to smile, and to jump with their legs all at different angles. Then I counted "One-two-three-jump!" and they jumped – all of them with good expressions and positions. It was not a difficult picture because they did exactly what I asked them to do. I began explaining to them how I wanted to portray this vivacity they radiated, and everything went fine from there. In fact, that was the beginning of when they started to realize that I knew what I was talking about photographically, because before then everybody photographed them just how they stood, or put them together anyhow.

'I'm always asked why I have such a comprehensive collection of pictures of the boys, especially as I was not even paid to take them on that scale . . . The main factor was that those boys completely overwhelmed me. They inspired me, and I was their slave! They didn't realize that, and I dared not let them know. I felt, suddenly, like a 17-year-old boy again, because of their attitude towards me and the whole photography thing.

There is no word to describe what happened between us; I only wish I were eloquent enough to describe those days, and all those little jokes and funny things that happened, because it is all still there in front of me. I stayed three whole days with them, long after the other *Record Mirror* staff had returned to London. I thought *Record Mirror* would sack me. Really, it was a labour of love.

'My relationship with them was unique. When I first met them I was old enough to be their father, and that age difference was important because photographically it helped me to get them to do what I wanted them to do. I was trained in the film industry to concentrate on photographing facial expressions and bring the best out of my subjects, and of course the Beatles were so obviously photogenic. But they were challenging subjects because they were four individual characters who couldn't stay still together long enough for me to photograph them as a foursome. At first it was impossible, but eventually I found the right medicine. . . .

'They had already had some marvellous pictures taken of them by Astrid Kirschner in Hamburg, and she introduced them to photography in a different type of way from how an English photographer would. But then they met me, and while Astrid was really an artist, a designer, I was an experienced photographer. It helped tremendously when the boys discovered my past work with artists in England, and my experiences before I came to England. By then I'd already photographed Presley, Sinatra, Monroe, Dietrich and everyone else from left, right and centre. The Beatles took full advantage of me, finding out about showbusiness, how to get in the press, how to handle the media, and all that sort of thing. After we became friends I told them, "Let's make sure we have enough pictures, because when you make it big, all the newspapers will want pictures straight away, and even if they have ten staff photographers, the picture editor will choose the freelance picture if it is better." And I was proved right.

'Now they had begun to respect me, and from this period they always had respect for photographers older than themselves. But as for the younger photographers, well, they didn't have quite so much respect for them. . . .

'There was one picture I took of John at Paul's house when he was half-dressing, putting on his shirt. And he hated it. He said, "Look, Dezo, you say you want clean-cut pictures of us, so why do you use this? I look like a tramp!"

'I replied, "Yes, but your face . . . I never saw you look so human as on this picture." And it's possible that this word "human" made him think, because eventually he loved that picture most, much better than the rest of the portraits. After that he always said, "Why didn't you get the rest of the shirt in the picture?"

'John liked everything where he didn't know he was being photographed. He hated being photographed. But although he may appear to be looking at the camera, it's not really *into* the camera, because he never knew when I photographed him. That was the technique I used. Whatever we did, at home, in hotels, in offices, in concerts, I would go from behind, or sideways, and I never told them what it was I was doing, so they never knew who I was after. Is it John? Is it all four of them? Is it Ringo – who on stage was always miles away at the back? They always let me do whatever I felt, because from experience I knew where that picture would eventually be usable.

'It's just like when you have any kind of learner, a tailor apprentice, or a shoemaker apprentice, or even a photographic apprentice – it takes him a long time to find his way. The Beatles had to learn the technique of how they should be photographed, and that's why they're so successful in their photographs. That's why there are so many books on them! I think I was the creator of that image; I don't want to dwell on it, but I was the Daddy of the thing.

'I would definitely give credit to my past experiences with the movie camera for certain aspects of my pictures, but the most distinctive aspect was that I only used flash under very exceptional circumstances. If I did, then I would do it in a sort of very funny way so that it was a bounce-light image. The flash would be far away from the camera, as in the photograph of the boys in the Cavern. I would be here with the camera, and the flash would be about fifteen yards away.

'I have the feeling that the whole secret of my pictures is that they are alive. They really are the split-second of that day, of that hour, of that month, of that year. It is just exactly how they were in that split-second.

'In London my offices were in Gerrard Street, but my studio was in Wardour Street, and when the Beatles arrived in London I took them there for some sessions. They already had plenty of fans in London, and when they found out where my studios were the place was besieged. Sometimes the Beatles would have to stay there for hours; my assistants would leave first and lock up, telling the fans that everyone had gone home. Then the boys would sneak out.

'One of the most famous sessions we did at the Wardour Street studios was with the collarless jackets, and I have the feeling these pictures are popular because the Beatles look pleasant and clean-cut. It is their first time in those "uniforms", without the stage and guitars making all sorts of wrinkles in their clothes, and there are all sorts of expressions. But the most popular one was – and still is – the picture where they are all smiling. That was their image. And however they looked later, beards, moustaches, that picture is still in the greatest demand. The collarless jackets were made by their tailor Douggie Millings, but the suggestion for the design came, I believe, from Germany, from Astrid and Stu, the Beatle who died.

'Whenever we did a session, I had to ask the boys to do everything twice – once for black-and-white, and once for colour. I took everything of the Beatles in black-and-white and colour. At that particular session I copied John French's idea of the white backgrounds. He was the top fashion photographer of that era, but I didn't have a chance to make the background in the same way. He would over-expose the white background to create the white, but I didn't have time because the groups would come in and out so quickly. In half an hour I had to make a session, black-and-white and colour, so I just lit up a white background. I did that picture of the four of them on the chair in about three minutes, but the session took me three months to organize. I would also project coloured backgrounds, but I never used the coloured paper background. That's why I always had gelatins of all sorts of colours. That's where the movie experience paid off very well again.

'They had some very good times in London, and I remember on one of the visits John had to sell his return ticket to Liverpool in order to stay one more day. That one fare was enough pocket-money for the rest of the boys. I'd often take them to lunch at the

Budapest Restaurant in Soho's Greek Street, and Paul's girlfriend Jane Asher would come with us; she liked Hungarian food. That's how it went in those days – we were living in each other's pockets. It was a good time, but in retrospect I must have neglected my studio tremendously, and my two assistants were in their element. They became the chief photographers in my absence. I was never in the studio because I was always out gallivanting with the Beatles, whether it was at the BBC Studios in Maida Vale, at Abbey Road or around town, Stowe School or wherever. I'm sorry now I didn't take pictures all the time. Then, I just took pictures while they were working.

'I did several other "jump" pictures with them; one was later on in Paris, but another was on the stage of the London Palladium at the time when the whole thing was just taking off for the boys. It was still very difficult to get colleagues from Fleet Street to photograph them. I would be begging them, but none of them really wanted to know. Some of them did it for my sake, but the Beatles weren't topping the bill. If they had been the Shadows, or that type of group . . . But "Beatles"? Everybody laughed.

'Later on, the photographers came and begged me, but by that time it was too late. The Beatles weren't interested. Anyway, when they were rehearsing on the Palladium stage we used a sort of tic-tac system we'd devised. It was really marvellous. I didn't need to shout: I just gesticulated and they jumped. Even up there they jumped in unison. When the other photographers saw what was going on, it magnetized them and they began crowding in, because nobody jumps on the Palladium stage with all their gear behind them. There's hardly any space to jump. But because we were lower down, the jump obviously looked higher, and a lot of photographers got similar pictures.

'By this time I was beginning to realize that the Beatles would penetrate the American market and would need more pictures. The ones I was taking then were to my mind not strong enough to catch the imagination of the American reader. The pictures had to be something special, because the Beatles were special.

'It was a few weeks before the time of their summer tour with Gerry and the Pacemakers when the idea came about to dress them in old-fashioned bathing costumes. I remember the occasion well and can pinpoint it as if it were today. George Martin was there and we had this split-second sort of idea – the kind you don't work on, it just comes, and then you expand on it. I told George that we must make the Beatles realize that eventually they will make it in the States and I want to be ahead with pictures, because by the time they make it it will be too late to take special pictures. You can't just send one picture to America – there must be a flow of them, a bombardment of different pictures. Of course, the boys didn't realize how big the USA was. You can't blame them.

'Epstein was dead against the bathing-costume idea, and so was John. Afterwards it occurred to me that John had visualized the bathing-costume sessions in the photographic studios, whereas my idea was to take them somewhere on location.

'"Leave it to me," I told them. "Every American newspaper will want to publish them." I chewed over the idea for several weeks and then I visited Berman's, the film and theatrical costumiers, and they had these bathing costumes in stock. I'd also visualized the session with old-fashioned bathing huts, but I couldn't locate any. I'd planned the session for Brighton beach, but the right time came during that summer tour at Weston-super-Mare on a hot, sunny day. The boys changed into the costumes in their van, and when they emerged they were like Tarzan – wild animals. They were suddenly free of everything. No worries – they were marvellous. You can see all this on the movie film I have of them. The size of the costumes didn't matter, and I hired some straw hats and they made some cut-out black beetles to fly like kites.

'I took a lot of pictures at Weston-super-Mare, and some of them were for the Typhoo Tea advertisement. Everything had been discussed through lawyers, and the agency sent me the letter shapes for T-Y-P-H-O-O made for the size of a $2\frac{1}{4}$-inch viewfinder; only the lettering was clear, the rest was blacked out. I had to fit the boys into the shapes of the lettering, and that's why we have them jumping off walls for the letter Y, etc. The whole session was done at Weston . . . I remember sitting on the grass discussing it after the deal had been finalized, and the boys said, "Let's do it around the hotel." They had to be wearing smart clothes, and it took me nearly the whole morning to do, because immediately they had to pose . . . well, they were much better when they were let loose. I had a lot of trouble with Ringo, just to get him to stand straight for the letter H, and as for their facial expressions! They just didn't realize what they looked like. And as I photographed them, they were using my movie camera to film each other. That's why I have this episode on the film.

'I stopped photographing the Beatles so frequently during 1964, and the reason was silly, really silly. I could kick myself because it sounds so childish. One morning I went to Twickenham film studios where the boys were already shooting for the third or fourth week on *Hard Day's Night*. I'd been quite busy on a tour with Cliff Richard and I was looking forward to seeing the Beatles again. When I got to the studio I saw John, and he was talking to a pretty girl. He was always talking to pretty girls! He saw me, and suddenly he became very angry and began ranting at me like I was his running boy. He completely lost control of himself in front of all those extras, electricians and cameramen; at that time I was the official of ACTT, the cinematographic union. He was angry because a picture of him had been published where his hair, blown by the wind, revealed his forehead. I had taken it in Miami while he was water-skiing. Now, the background story to this picture is that every time I went somewhere, I always got assignments from papers which paid me in advance, and in this case I was paid by *Tit-Bits*. The Beatles, or NEMS, never paid me for pictures, even though they used them all over the world. As soon as I got back from America I sent *Tit-Bits* the pictures immediately I printed them, everything from everywhere, so they had about twelve pages of pictures of the Beatles in America – a lovely feature – and John picked on that one picture. I still think it's a lovely picture, full of life, as if he's saying, "Look, I can ski already!" The instructor was not even holding him. John couldn't understand why I released this picture because before then I never released anything I believed was not really their image. That was the point, and he was hurt. Yet that picture was one of the best from the whole clip.

'I felt so humiliated in front of all those people that I couldn't even answer him. I just turned my back on him and walked out. And I obviously finished with the Beatles also. In my imagination I had thought of myself as a father figure to them, and I couldn't believe that John could talk to me as if I were a 6-year-old kid.

'Just after this incident, while they were still filming, the president of *Cash Box* and his wife came to present them with four globes for their American chart successes. The presentation was in the canteen of the Twickenham studios, and was a most terrifying experience for me because not only were the Americans good friends of mine, but I was also the official *Cash Box* photographer in London. There was no other photographer at the ceremony and when John saw me he got mad. I could see it in his face. The other boys had to calm him down and I actually have the picture of it. Every time I see it I nearly get sick – I didn't want to take those pictures but I had to. I couldn't send my assistant because of the President of *Cash Box*, and I had to go myself. It was such a silly scene but luckily no one noticed it, only the other boys, and they knew the score.

'There was another incident between us while the boys were

rehearsing at the Prince of Wales Theatre for their Christmas show that year. I was covering the event when their press guy, Derek Taylor, came up to me and said, "Dezo, I feel so awkward because he doesn't want you at the press reception. He said he doesn't want to see you." I replied that I didn't want to see him either, so I quickly returned to the office and sent my assistant, who got the pictures.

'There is a happy aftermath to all this which happened in the 'seventies. I was in New York, at the Plaza, and I got a 'phone call. This was strange because I didn't realize anyone knew I was there. John was on the line. It really shook me – how he knew I was there I don't know, but he said that he was so pleased I was in New York, and can I come over to his flat, it's not very far. I said to myself, "What on earth is going on?"

'When I arrived at his apartment he had a beard and looked terribly neglected. This was during that period he had split from Yoko, but apparently he had just turned up on their doorstep. He didn't mention anything about the split with Yoko, and didn't mention anything about our private business together all those years before. He was just enquiring about London and everybody around, and what was new, and after we spoke for a while he began talking to Yoko indirectly through me. She was in the same room and I realized they were not on speaking terms. He was using me as a middle-man. Anyway, I quickly found an excuse to leave, but I'm really glad I went to see him, because we made up our very good friendship. He kissed me when we parted.

'Even today, I still think the break was my fault, that I was wrong in turning my back on him and walking away, but I had been hurt at being treated like a young boy. John never mentioned it, and I never mentioned it, but probably he was thinking about it. He wouldn't even acknowledge it. He was that sort of character.

'He knew how wounding he could be, and he was not only like that with me, but also with the other Beatles, with Brian, with Neil and Mal. But he regretted all those things later, and in my case he certainly must have done otherwise he wouldn't have invited me over. That fitted him to apologize, or something. That was his way of making peace.

'John was a very interesting character; he could be your best pal, but he could also be a Jekyll and Hyde; you never knew when he'd turn his venom against you. One day he would be sweet, the next day he'd jump at you and bite. That didn't just apply to outsiders, but to everybody, even to his wife Cynthia. John was consistent in that respect. Really, I think it was self-defence, something that was born in him. I put everything down to insecurity with him. Yet he was an enigma because although he was insecure, he was also very self-confident. I can't explain that.

'He was a very strong-minded person and sometimes too much so for his own good. During a gold disc presentation ceremony, he even started to argue with the managing director of Capitol Records, and John didn't even know who he was. Even Brian Epstein was sometimes afraid to knock on the dressing-room or hotel-room door, because he didn't know what sort of mood John would be in that day.

'I never came across that type of moody behaviour in a young chap of that age before, but much of it was due to the pressures of success. During the first year I worked with the Beatles, these traits were never evident. And at the height of the pressures of success, John could change his moods so quickly. For example, when we travelled to America for the first time, on the flight over John had an unpleasant argument with the rest of the boys, and they really weren't seeing eye to eye. They were travelling first-class and weren't mixing with the press and business people in the tourist class. I came up to see them, but when I felt that tension I returned to my own seat and didn't interfere. But once they landed at Kennedy Airport and came into the VIP lounge for the press conference, the four of them were completely together again. From being so moody in the morning, John became an angel. He couldn't have behaved better. And without John, that trip wouldn't have been such a huge national success – he was the driving force. It was John who led the Beatles' conquest of America.

'He was always acknowledged as leader by the other Beatles and Brian; he had that leadership charisma, that gangland type of thing. It was born in him. He stuck out to me as leader from the moment I met him at Epstein's office in Liverpool. He had that sort of arrogant air – he was the boss.

'John's outlook on life was basically left-wing, and it was reinforced by some of the things he saw in America. During the Miami trip, by the swimming-pool at the Deauville Hotel, every five minutes there would be a fashion parade with models telling guests where they could buy the clothes and for how much. And although it was terribly hot, certain women guests would keep appearing in fur coats – just to show off – and John couldn't comprehend it. He started making jokes about it and they were so funny, unbelievably funny. He was also flabbergasted at the food at the hotel. "One of those meals," he would say, "would be enough for a whole family in England for a day."

'He also observed that the waiters, mostly Cuban immigrants, were very careful with the heaps of leftovers on the plates; the food would be going back with them for their families.

'Later, when he wrote songs with more social awareness, many of his sentiments went back to that period. But obviously, he couldn't directly offend people. He knew that whatever he wrote, however he wrapped it up, would pinpoint a certain area or occasion. Both John and Paul were very clever when it came to songs, but generally Paul was much more level-headed.

'John was always for the underprivileged, for the Third World, and for the people in England. But the funny thing was that he would never do anything for the poor people in Liverpool. It was a complete paradox, especially when you compare him with Jesus Christ, as he sometimes did himself. He was a most contradictory type of character because he financed the British Black Power leader Michael X; Yoko had convinced John to give money to Michael X and for a long time he was living lavishly on John Lennon's money, big money. And John had the cheek to let himself be persuaded by Yoko to go on a television show and parade this Michael X, who was already very well known by Scotland Yard and officialdom. Later, Michael was hung for murder in Jamaica.

'You could come to John and tell him you were in a terrible state, that your firm was bankrupted or whatever, and he'd give you £10,000 – even if he didn't know you. But on the other hand, if *I'd* gone up to him and said, "I don't have enough for lunch," he wouldn't have given me a penny.

'John was brought up to look after himself in every respect; he'd had all sorts of bad experiences and as he became more famous he wanted to avoid them. He knew from when he met people how they would try to skim him; he was terribly aware of the money side. I think that when their success came, John was a bit disappointed in the scheme of things because they became so big so fast. He could have been successful at whatever he turned his hand to. He could have been an artist in his own right, especially after all the influence Stu had on him. He was always doodling; every restaurant, every napkin, was doodled up with words and pictures. I only wish I had kept them all.

'John was different. He was an extrovert. You can't really describe him because he behaved according to how he felt. You could write a whole book about his complex personality . . . but I couldn't write that book. That's why I only photographed.'

From an interview with Dezo Hoffmann during early 1985

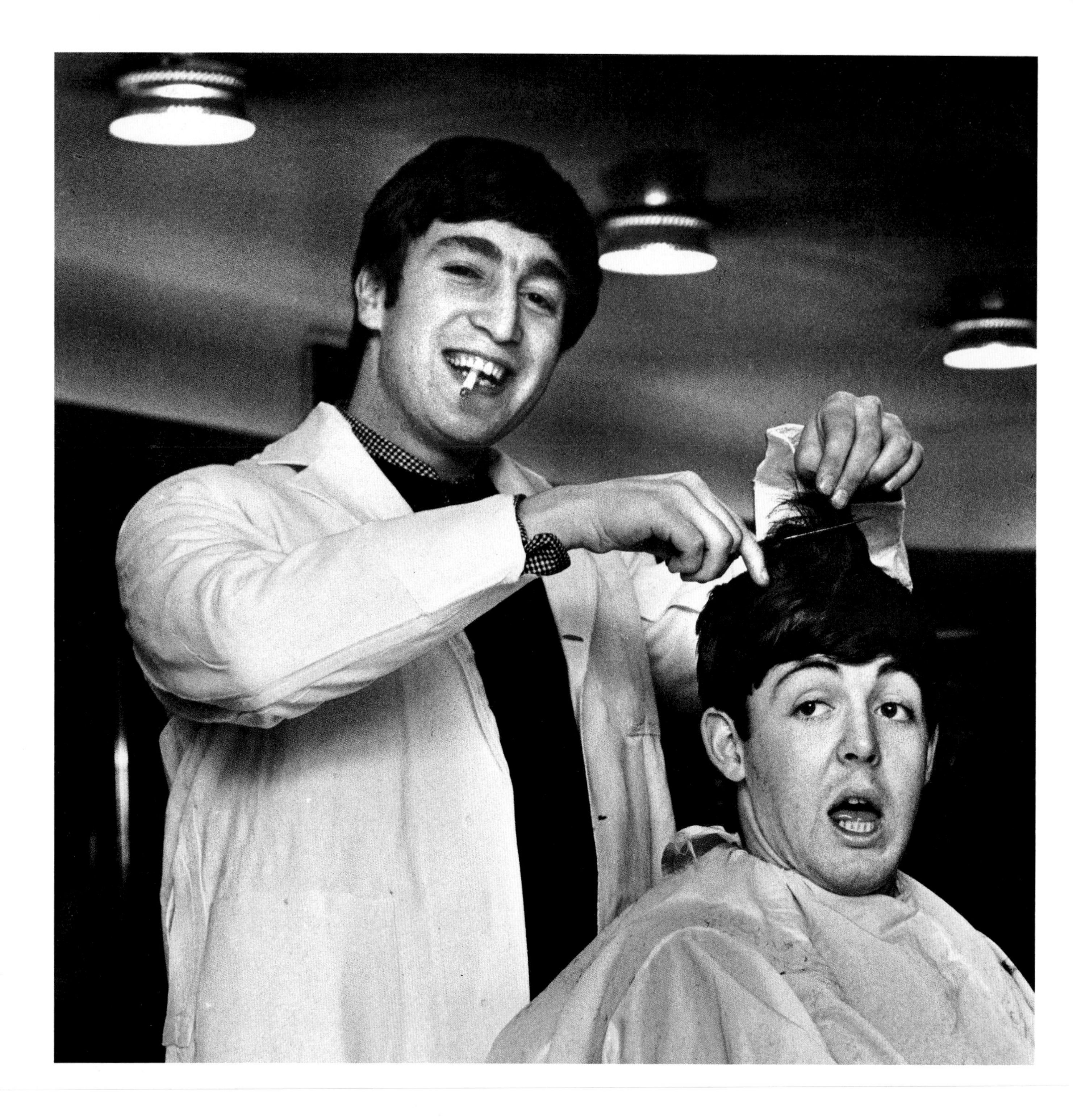

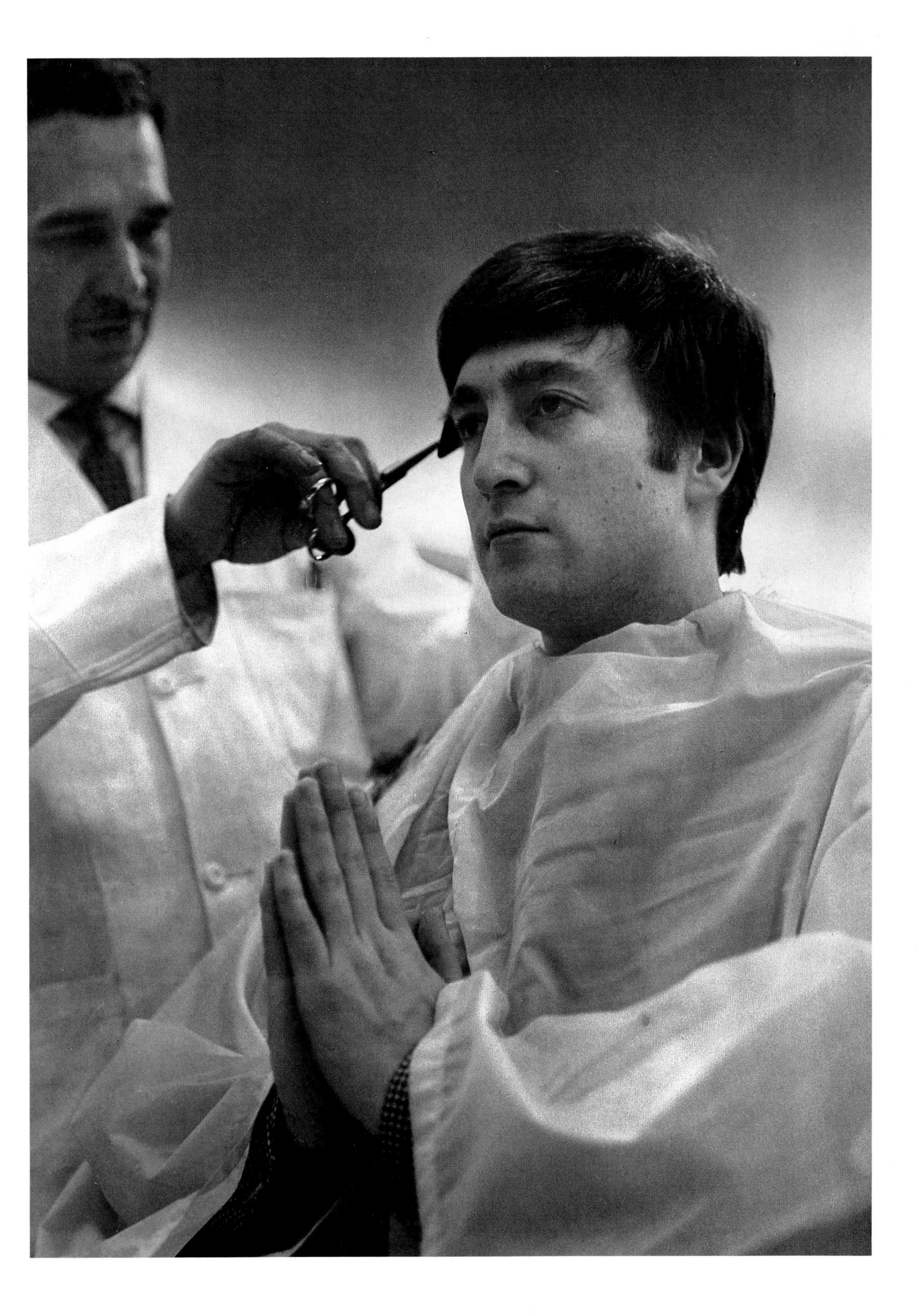

1

RAILWAYS
CARLTON
STREET
British Railways
travel centre
R.Mace Ltd
2. ST MARY Rd

Rickenbacker

Gibson

25 | 26 | 27

30

32

33 | 34 | 35

TLE

Rickenbacker

Rickenbacker

43 | 44 | 45

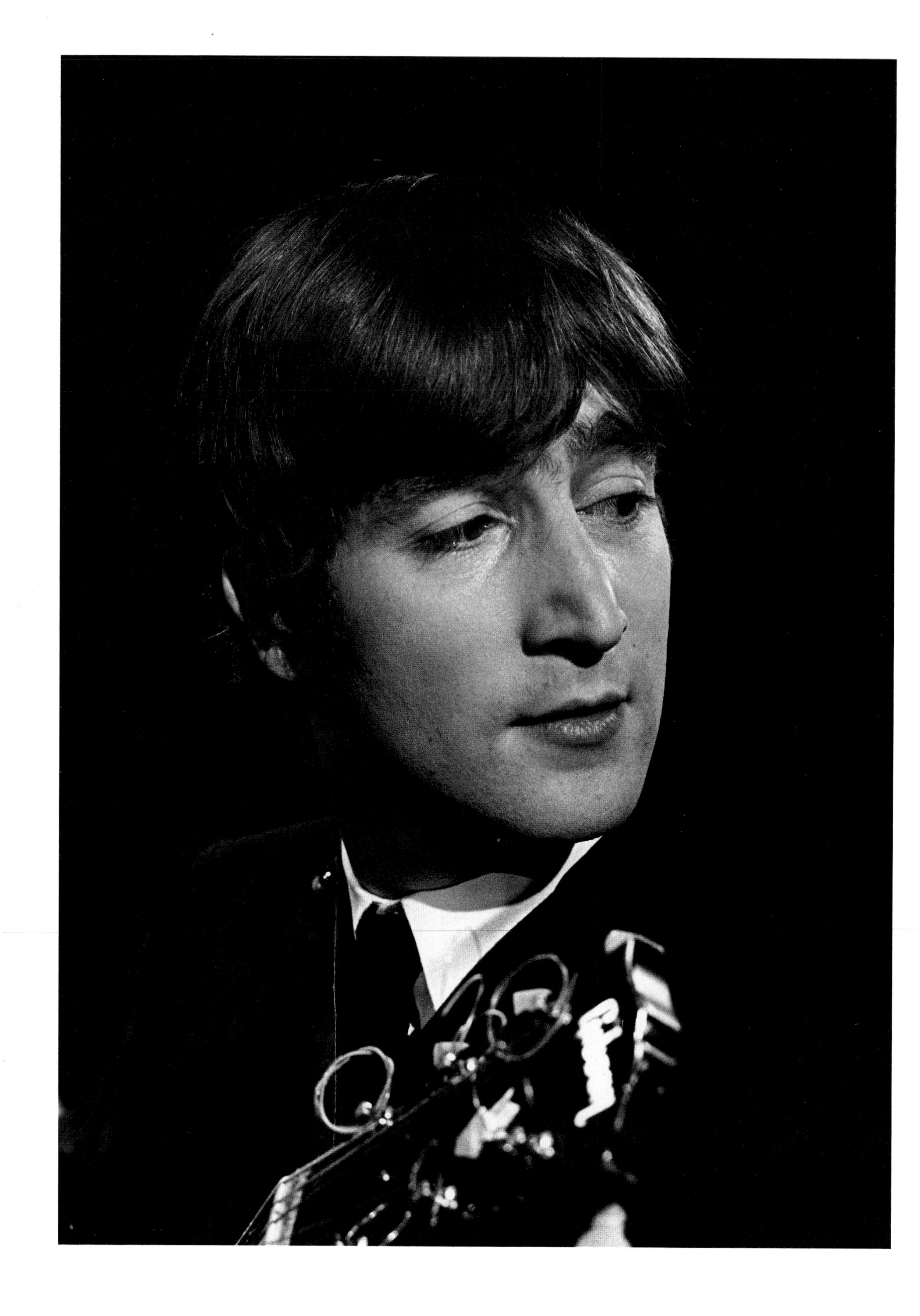

48

47

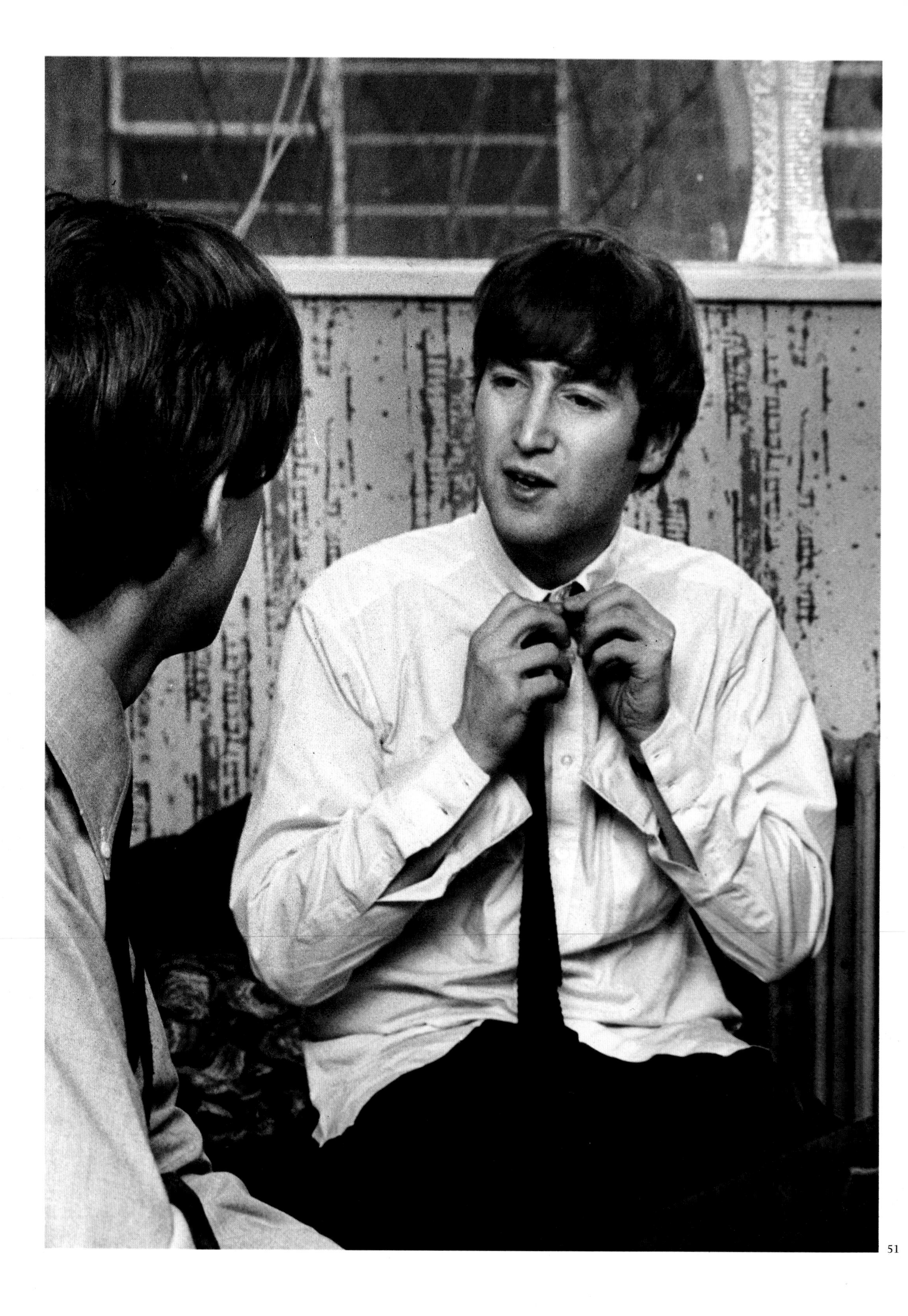

MISS
JOHN
LENNON

Letters to the
MICHAEL FRAYN
LA TROPICAL

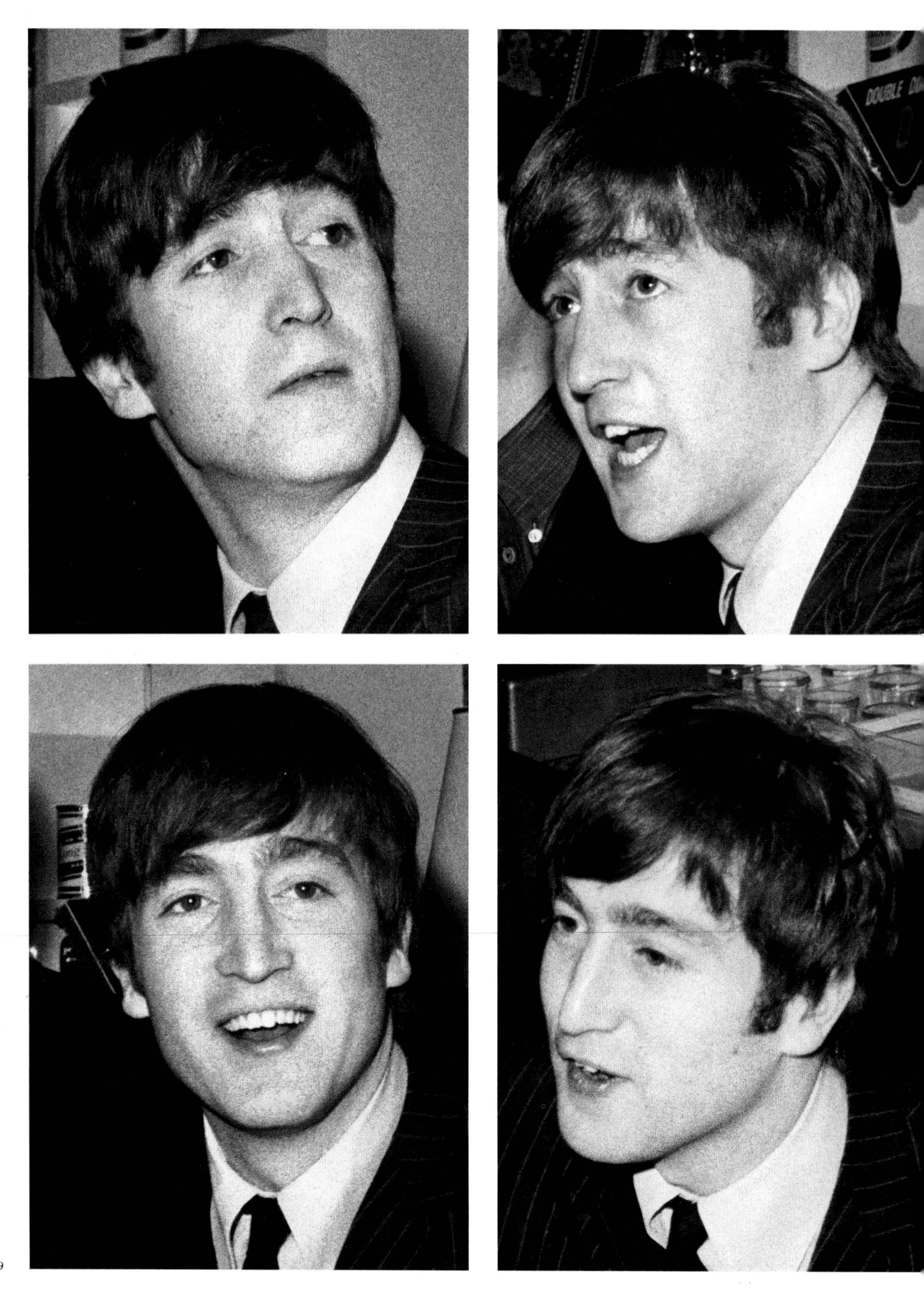

LONG LIFE 1/3
LIGHT 1/4
BROWN 1/6
SPECIAL STOUT
JOHN BULL 1/
1/8
ARCTIC
LAGER 1/
GUINNESS 1/2
CIDER OR SHANDY
2/6
2/3
RUM 2/9
2/9
ORANGE 3/-
ERMOUTH 2/9
SHERRY
VARIOUS 3/6
1/2
8

THE
BEATL

MAISON CATHERINE
BOULANGERIE
LA MERE
CATHERINE
RESTAURANT

78

77 | 79

1963
REVIEW
Cash Box
MUSIC
&
RECORDS
PART ONE
MUSIC
&
RECORDS
INTERNATIONAL
PART TWO
COIN MACHINE
&
VENDING
PART THREE

PAN AM

PA

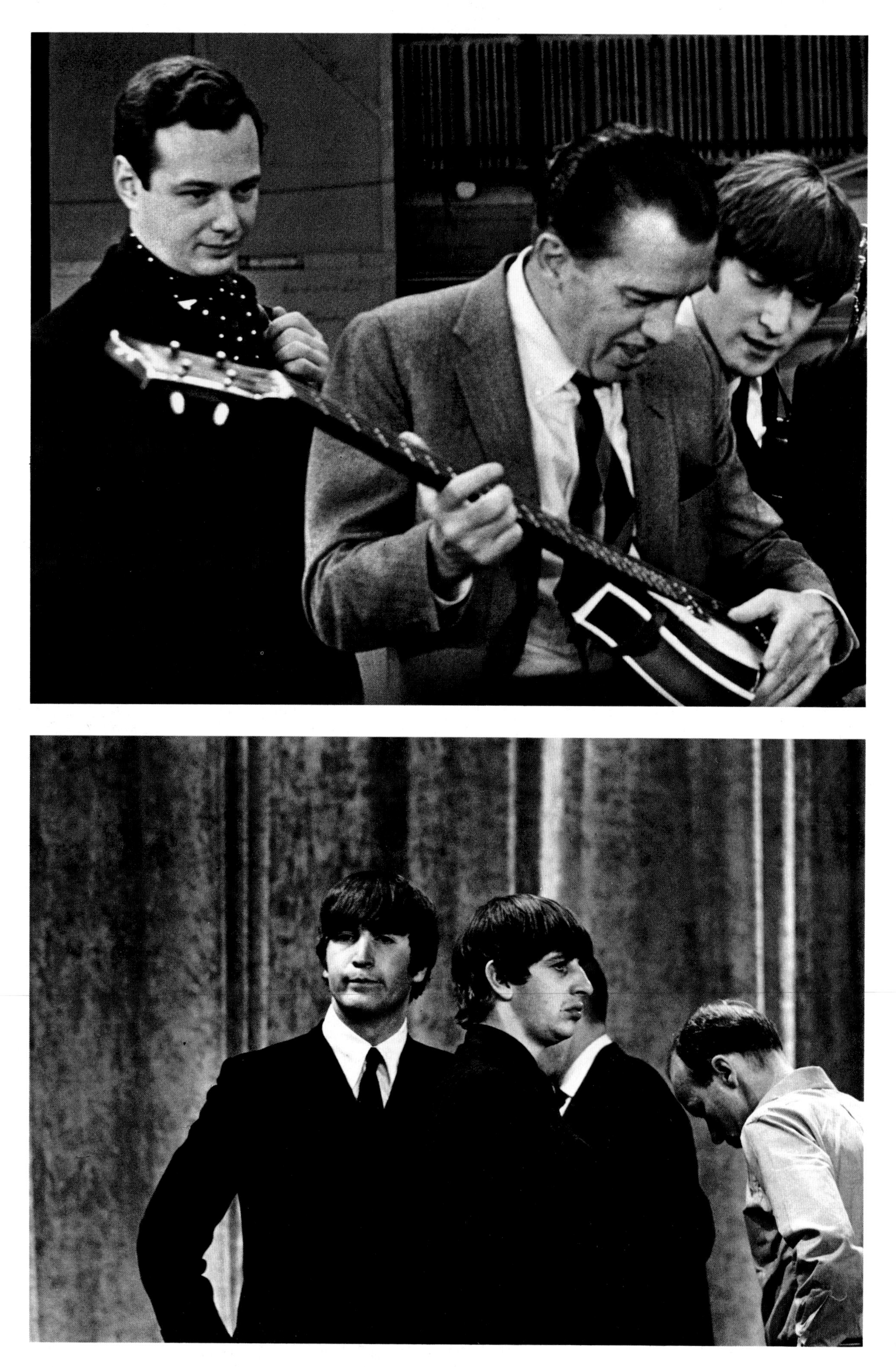

88

89

A FULL CIRCLE OF MUSIC AND SOUND
EPIC
RECORDS
COLUMB
RECOR
COLUMB
RECO
COLUMB

93→

EPIC
Records

A FULL CIRCLE OF MUSIC AND SOUND
KEEP AWAY FROM HEAT
Macy's

Coke
7up
Coke

VOX
VOX
THE
BEATLES

Rickenbacker

THE BEATLES
BRITISH EUROPEAN

118 →

WELCOME HOME BOYS
15

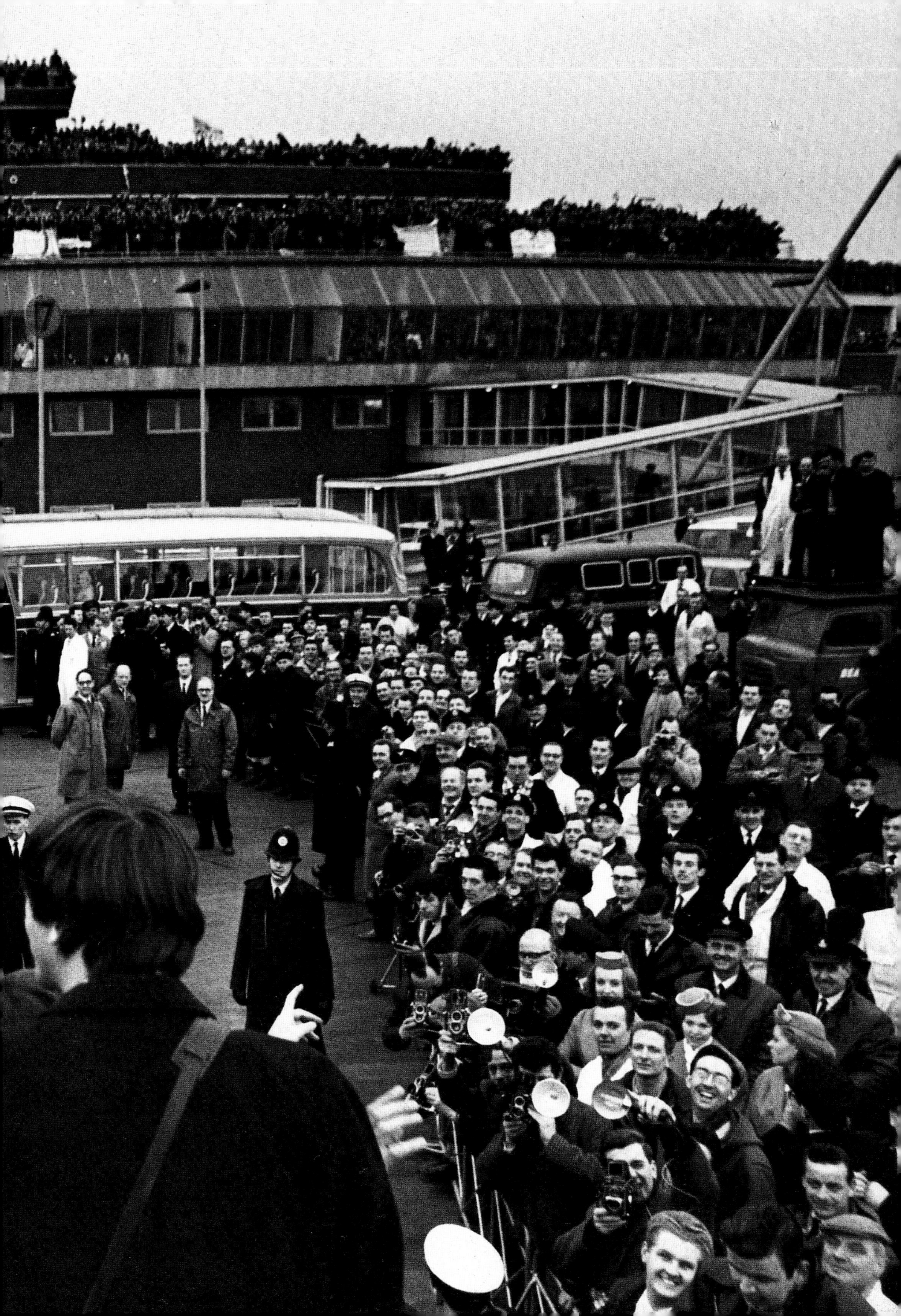

VOX

120 | 121

122 →

VOX

123–126

130

131

Rickenbacker

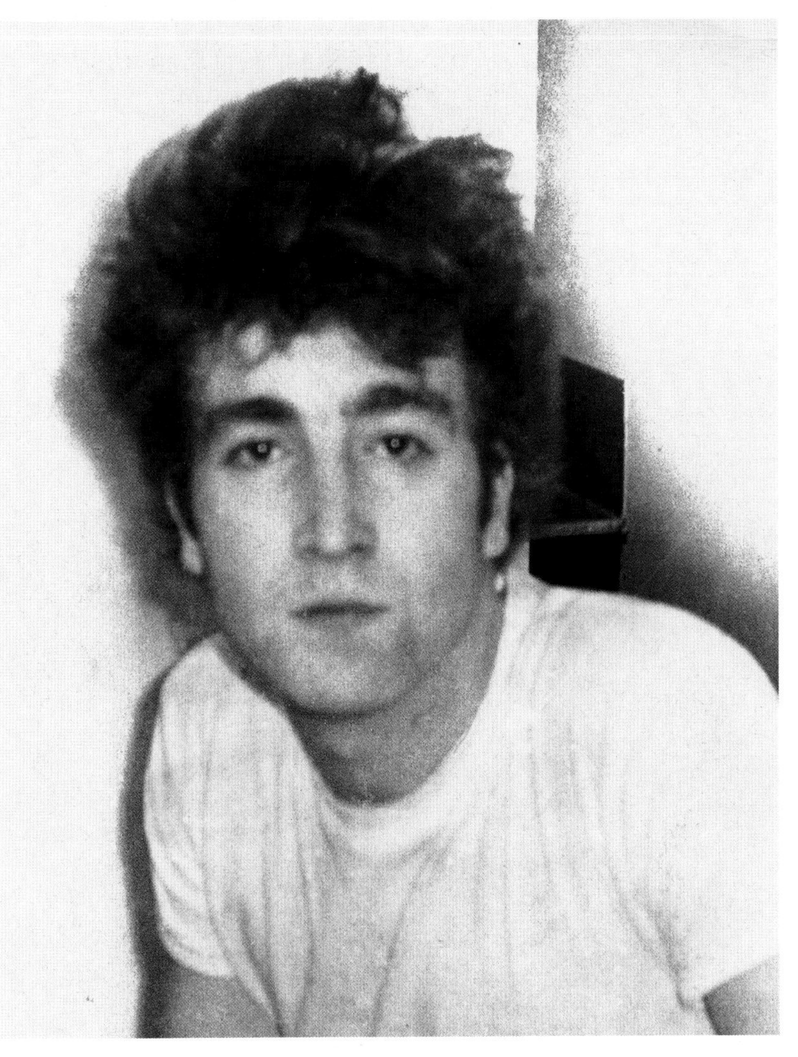

139

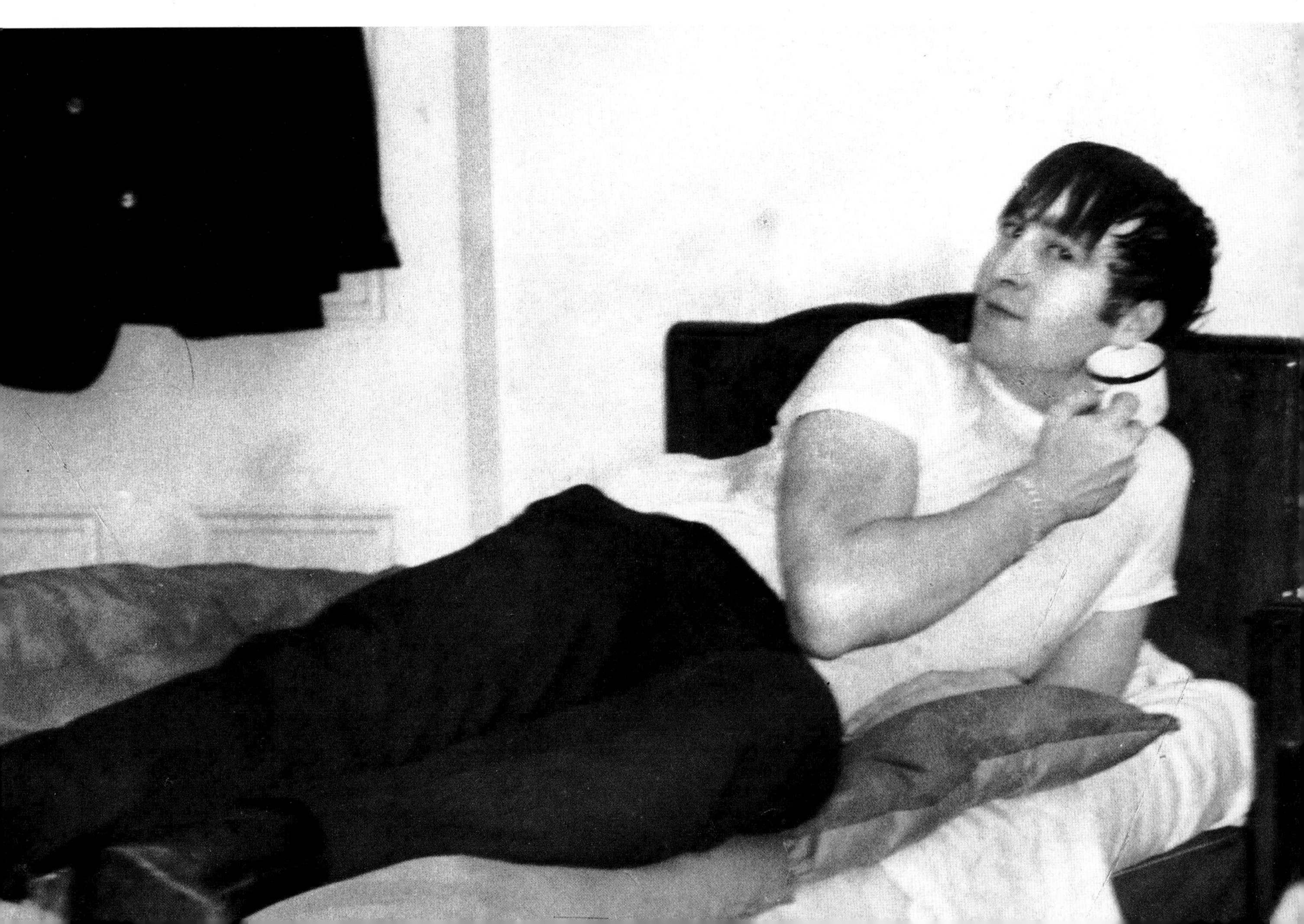

EAGLE

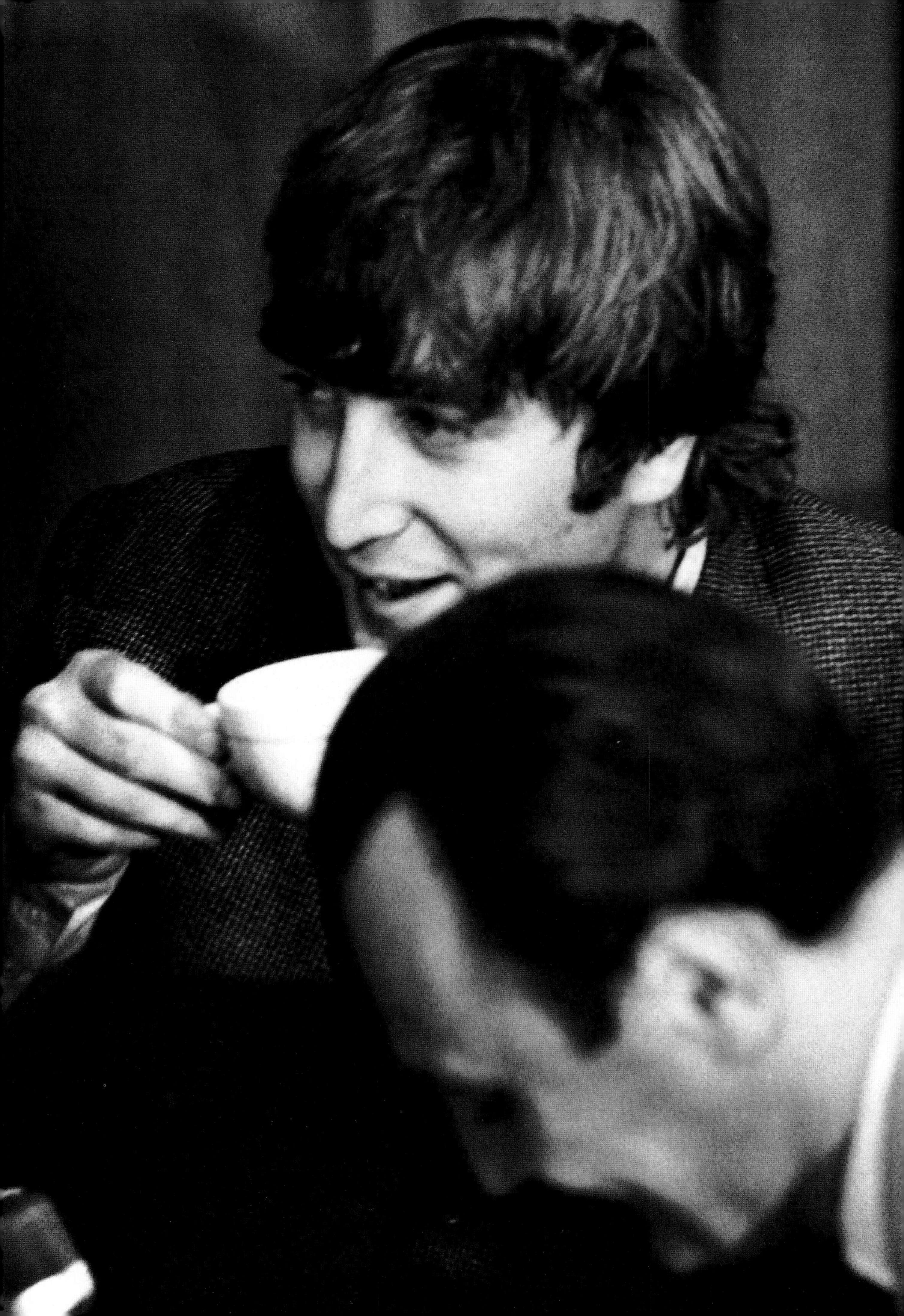

146 | 147 | 148

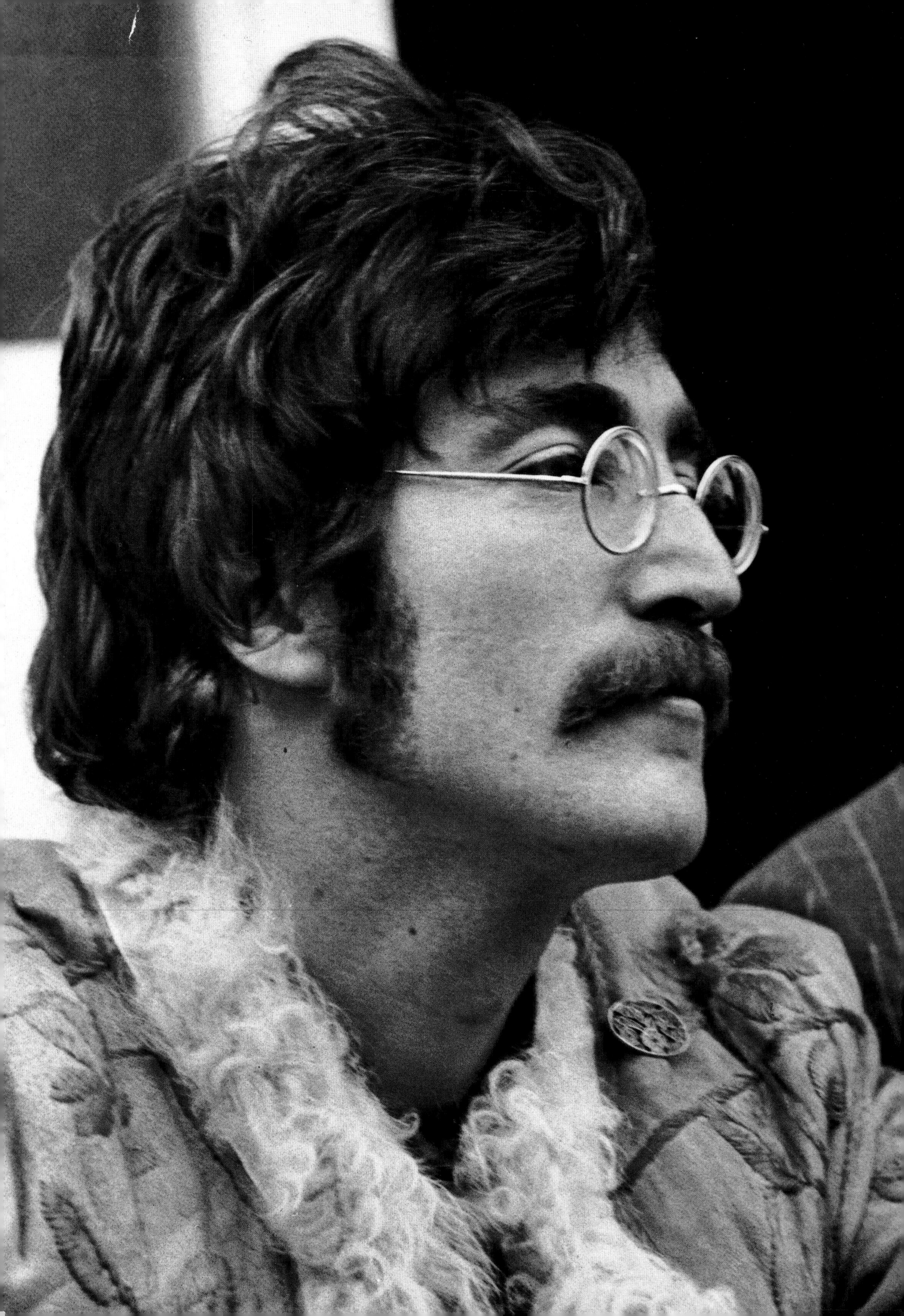

IS
EST
RAUCHT

CAPTIONS

Selection of Polyfotos, 9 October 1944
(1) When I published the first Beatles picture book in 1963, it was my intention to include some early photographs so their fans would know how they looked when they were children. All the boys sent me snaps, but unfortunately none arrived in time for publication. These Polyfotos of John, aged four, are from a large sheet containing several dozen which I purchased from John's Aunt Mimi. Three or four had already been snipped off and given to friends or relatives in Liverpool.

EMI Studios, 11 September 1962
(2) The Beatles' first recording session for Parlophone produced by George Martin at the Abbey Road studios in St John's Wood. St John, serious and concentrated, is seen working on 'Love Me Do', on which St Paul took the lead vocal. The other track recorded at this session was 'PS I Love You'.

EMI Studios, 4 March 1963
(3) On the entrance steps of Abbey Road studios during a break in recording. An EMI photographer is setting up his plate camera for a possible album-cover shot. **(4)** John and Ringo listening to the playback of 'Thank You Girl' in the control room of Number One studio. **(5)** It was actually George Martin's idea to colour up 'From Me To You' with harmonica.

Liverpool, April 1963
(6) Jumping for joy in Sefton Park after the success of 'Please Please Me'. **(7)** Leaning against the wall of Paul's house and looking out on to the back garden in the mild spring sunshine. **(8, 9)** The original idea for their mop-top look was conceived by Stu Sutcliffe's German girlfriend Astrid Kirschner, but eventually the boys convinced their local Liverpool barber to sculpt their hair in the 'new' style. They visited him every week in the basement hairdressing salon at Dunn's mens' shop. **(10)** John gives me a grin that says, 'We did it!' Pressure from their home-town audience had forced promoters Arthur Howes and Eve Taylor to rearrange their concert-tour billing; in Liverpool, at least, the Beatles topped the bill, stealing the show from American stars Chris Montez and Tommy Roe. **(11)** After our exhausting photographic session, John relaxes, braces down, and pours himself a cuppa in Paul's kitchen.

BBC Paris Cinema, London, April 1963
(12) A rare shot of John at that time with glasses. If he had noticed me with the camera he would have taken them off, but he was so engrossed in working out a melody with Paul that he was oblivious to the click of my camera. **(13)** In the dressing-room of the Paris Cinema, Lower Regent Street; this is the photograph of John that at first he hated, then grew to love. **(14)** Clowning around by the British Railway Travel Centre, next to the Paris Cinema, just before the live lunchtime broadcast.

Stowe Grammar School, April 1963
(15) 'What, no girls?' John was completely flabbergasted to arrive at Stowe and find himself surrounded by a new breed of fan – English public schoolboys. Any Beatles' preconceptions about public school snobbery were shattered at the warm and friendly welcome they received from pupils and staff alike. And at the concert that evening, there was no screaming and shouting – only civilized appreciation – and because they could actually hear themselves play, the boys really let it rip.

Cecil Gee's, London, April 1963
(16) The boys had always dreamed of owning clothes from Cecil Gee, one of London's top 'gents' outfitters', as they used to be called, and their ambitions were quickly satisfied. Here's John choosing a pair of trousers with a little help from Paul.

Royal Albert Hall, London, 9 May 1963
(17) The only time the Beatles ever played at the Albert Hall was for the BBC's *Swinging Sound '63*, a packed programme also featuring Del Shannon, Susan Maugham, the Springfields, Chris Barber, the Vernons Girls and Shane Fenton. Wearing his brand-new collarless jacket, John takes lead vocals on 'Please Please Me'.

Dezo Hoffmann's photographic studio, London, April 1963
(18) This was the first time the boys had been in my own studio in Wardour Street, and the photograph shows John in one of their new outfits. **(19)** A close-up of John in the suit made for him by Soho tailor Douggie Millings.

Dezo Hoffmann's photographic studio, London, June 1963
(21) It was around this time that John first started to be photographed in glasses. It took me a long time to find an optician locally, but eventually I bought some frames with no glass in them so he could see how he looked in the mirror. We only had the one frame and we did all sorts of pictures. (20) One of the pictures was a self-exposure. I purposely put the camera on a tripod and told him, 'If you want the picture, do it yourself, because I have to photograph the other boys.' So he did it himself.

EMI Studios, July 1963
(22) John in the no. 2 studio during the 'All My Loving' session, talking to George Martin in the control room. (23) I purposely took this picture to show George Martin's characteristic way of holding his finger against his eardrum in order to hear the pitch more clearly.

London, July 1963
(24) Waiting for an assistant at a chemist's shop (now a strip club) in Brewer Street, Soho. (25, 26) Buying bananas in Soho's Berwick Market. Note the prices. (27) Tea and ciggies yet again, but this time at the President Hotel in Bloomsbury Square. This was the first time the Beatles could afford to stay in a hotel.

Weston-super-Mare, July 1963
(28) John was seldom as happy-go-lucky as the time he wore this Edwardian bathing costume on the beach at Weston-super-Mare, a seaside resort in Somerset. I arranged this session especially for the American market, which I was certain the Beatles would soon break into. This was during their first bill-topping tour, which also starred Roy Orbison and Gerry and the Pacemakers. (29) Spontaneously jumping over George and thoroughly enjoying himself. (30) Posing as a circus strongman. (31) He was like Tarzan returning to the jungle after being in 'civilization'. Here he's watched by Les Maguire of the Pacemakers. (32) The boys' interpretation of what a Beatle (beetle?) looks like. They cut them out themselves and brought them from Liverpool. (33, 34) Two contrasting modes of transport; taking it easy on Eddie, the seaside donkey, and about to negotiate a hairpin bend on a go-kart, at that time the latest craze. (35) Relaxing in the sun lounge of their bed-and-breakfast boarding house.

London Palladium, 13 October 1963
(36) In those days, to top the bill on *Sunday Night at The London Palladium* was the pinnacle of showbusiness success. It was around this time that Beatlemania was beginning to sweep Britain, and this was the boys' first appearance at the Palladium.

EMI House, Manchester Square, November 1963
(37, 38, 39) They performed a few songs for the crowds of journalists, photographers and freeloaders gathered to see them receive their Silver Disc for the *Please Please Me* album.

***Royal Variety Performance*, London Palladium, 4 November 1963**
These shots were all taken at the rehearsals. On the actual night a star-studded audience, including the Queen Mother, Princess Margaret and Lord Snowdon stamped the seal of royal approval on their career. (40) John and Paul make no secret of a disagreement. (41) John on stage. (42) During a break. (43) John shares a joke with Tommy Steele, by now the classic 'all-round entertainer'. (44) Backstage encouragement from Brian Epstein.

Granada TV Studios, Manchester, November 1963
(45, 46, 47) This was the first that the Beatles had been in a TV studio for their own programme; it was a Beatles special produced by Johnny Hamp and these shots were taken during the rehearsals. (48) A cameraman explains the technicalities of a Granada TV camera.

***The Morecambe & Wise Show*, ATV Studios, Elstree, 2 December 1963**
(49) Eric and Ernie were worried that the Beatles might be nervous; John, on the other hand, was concerned that Morecambe & Wise might be nervous with the now-famous Beatles guesting on their show. (50) John in action on the *Morecambe & Wise Show*. (51) Back in the dressing-room changing for the next scene. (52) Relaxing in the dressing-rooms. (53) Striking a Napoleonic pose in boater and blazer for the benefit of my camera. (54) 'No, Ernie,' says Eric. 'They're only going to play their instruments. They won't be telling any jokes, you don't have to worry . . .'

***Juke Box Jury*, Liverpool, 11 December 1963**
(55) Silhouetted against the train window on the trip up to Liverpool. This was the first time the popular BBC-TV show *Juke Box Jury* had been televised outside London. (56) John gives the thumbs-down to some unlucky recording artist. The 'misses' on that particular programme were records by Paul Anka, Shirley Ellis, and the Blossoms. (57) In the comfort of a British Rail First Class compartment, John reads the morning paper on the way up to Liverpool. (58) Arriving at the station.

Wimbledon Palais, 14 December 1963
(59) Some of John's different moods as he meets three thousand fans who shook their hands, kissed their hands, fainted, touched their hair and even tried to leap over the barriers, braving the dozen or so attendants standing by. The occasion was titled 'The Southern Area Fan Club Get-together' and all it cost a Beatle fan was a mere three shillings and sixpence – $17\frac{1}{2}$p! (60, 61) The hard-core Beatlemaniacs were fenced in like football fans. Nobody could hear the boys play for the din, and even the girls selling souvenirs were forced to wear ear-plugs. (62) Shortly before going on stage, John looks very self-satisfied at having met all the fans and survived. Notice the drink prices. (63) Onstage, inaudible.

EMI Studios, December 1963
(64) Abbey Road studio no. 2 was converted to a reception area where the EMI artists and their entourages could gather. It wasn't altogether John's cup of tea; his moods would swing from one extreme to the other.

The Beatles Christmas Show, London, December 1963
(65, 66, 67) That year there was a special Beatles' Christmas show, held at the Astoria, Finsbury Park. It had, after all, been the year of the Beatles. Hosted by Rolf Harris and featuring artists such as Cilla Black and Billy J. Kramer, it didn't matter at all whether the Beatles sang or indulged in comedy routines. Their contributions were, as always, drowned out in screams.

Paris, January 1964
(68, 69) En route to Paris for their first Continental appearances since the Hamburg Star Club era – but this time it was all considerably more up-market; a three-week season at the Olympia Theatre, Paris, staying at Europe's most expensive hotel, the famous George V. **(70)** When the news broke that 'I Want To Hold Your Hand' was in the American charts, I rushed to the US embassy in Paris, borrowed a huge stars-and-stripes and hung it up over a window to use as appropriate background for a photo session. **(71, 72)** Along the Left Bank at Montmartre; John mingled with the painters and sometimes admired their work. **(73)** It was a bitterly cold day and we went into a bistro where a very attractive young lady served us coffee. I asked her to pose outside with the boys, and even though she'd never heard of them she changed into flimsy French postcard-style clothes. It only took me three minutes to get the shots, but by then she was blue with cold, despite John snuggling up against her from the back. **(74)** In the forecourt of the Hotel George V, surrounded by stone nymphs. **(75)** Arriving backstage at the dressing-room of the Olympia. **(76)** Enjoying a large mouthful of the newly-discovered crêpes suzettes, which became the boys' staple diet during their stay in Paris. The crêpes were so hot John had trouble swallowing them. **(77, 79)** Onstage at the Olympia. The audience was mostly male, and very appreciative of the Beatles' musicianship. **(78)** '*Salut*' at Orly airport. **(80)** The issue of *Cash Box*, the American music trade weekly, that first showed the Beatles at no. 1 in the singles chart with 'I Want To Hold Your Hand'. **(81)** I was involved in an Australian Apples promotion, and I had already photographed everyone else who was to be featured in the promotion – including the three other Beatles. But it wasn't until Paris that I had the chance to photograph John with an apple. The soft-focus effect wasn't deliberate; it was only later that I discovered Ringo had handled the camera and left a sticky fingermark from a crêpe suzette on the lens.

Heathrow Airport, London, 7 February 1964
(82) 'Give my regards to Broadway . . .' Jussy Antall, London editor of the Swedish newspaper *Expressen*, bids John goodbye and good luck at Heathrow's VIP lounge.

Kennedy Airport, New York, February 1964
(83) Our view from the aircraft as we stopped and saw the fans massing on the observation platforms with 'Beatles 4 Ever' welcome placards, and the droves of accredited photographers and newsmen. **(84)** John Winston Lennon's finest hour. He really excelled himself in the Press Lounge at their first American conference. I watched amazed as several hundred hard-boiled reporters who had come to destroy the Beatles ended up adoring them.

Central Park, New York, February 1964
(85) After a couple of days in New York the Beatles were beginning to get recognized. Here's John taking the reins of one of Central Park's famous fiacres.

Ed Sullivan Show, New York, February 1964
(86) A happy Ed Sullivan greets John and very nearly greets Neil Aspinall as 'George' . . . John had to explain that Neil (the real 'fifth Beatle') was standing in at rehearsals for the real George, who was still sick back at the Plaza Hotel. Seen behind Neil is Beatles' road manager Mal Evans, later shot dead in error by police in Los Angeles. **(87)** In full swing on the *Ed Sullivan Show*. **(88)** Three immortals from different areas of the music business – Brian Epstein, Ed Sullivan and John Lennon, who looks on with interest as Ed tries to figure out the intricacies of Paul's left-handed bass guitar. **(89)** John and Ringo deep in thought during the intermission; not in their wildest dreams could they have guessed they were stopping teenage crime on America's streets for one whole night. They were later congratulated on this achievement by a high-ranking police officer. **(90)** I would have loved to have read John's thoughts as he was preparing to perform on the Sullivan show.

Plaza Hotel, New York, February 1964
(91, 93) The Beatles' suite (the whole of the Plaza's twelfth floor) was an Aladdin's cave full of gifts, chocolates, and their favourite albums, sent free by courtesy of America's incredulous record industry, which they were about to turn upside-down. **(92)** Breakfast at the Plaza; Cynthia and John hide behind dark glasses while George, now on the mend, chats to his sister Louise who had flown in from Illinois to join him but soon became his nurse. In the mirror Paul can be seen talking to top New York DJ Murray the K, who had already dubbed himself 'the fifth Beatle'. **(94)** At the Beatles' second American press conference, held at the Plaza's Baroque Rooms, John hovers behind top TV syndicated psychologist Dr Joyce Brothers, who publicly analyzed the Beatles' enormous appeal to American teenagers. **(95)** The Plaza Press Conference, containing all of America's top newspaper and TV reporters, newsreel cameramen, radio announcers and a large international contingent. By this time the boys had perfected their delivery of witty one-liners, and the whole show was held together with military precision by their press officer Brian Sommerville, who had formerly been an officer in the Royal Navy and knew how to exert strict discipline.

New York to Washington, 11 February 1964
(96) Dismounting from the Edwardian-era luxury coach that had been added on to the regular New York–Washington train for the Beatles' benefit. I nearly broke my neck in the overall pandemonium at Washington's Union Station walking backwards taking pictures of the entourage moving along the platform. It proved impossible for the official welcoming committee led by Carroll James (the First American DJ to play 'I Want To Hold Your Hand') to greet them off the train. The crowd was all reporters and cameramen; no fans had been allowed on the platform. In the excitement I even left my precious astrakhan hat on the train; it was returned to me later by the station master. **(97)** George Martin and John relaxing en route to Washington. **(98)** Cynthia was now wearing a black wig to disguise herself. She was shy and hated the limelight. **(99)** A view of the whole carriage, with John at the centre of attention.

Washington Coliseum, 11 February 1964
(100, 101, 102, 103) This was the Beatles' first live concert in the States and the boys had never enjoyed themselves so much. The noise was absolutely ear-splitting and they were lucky to escape injury from all the jelly beans pelting the stage. They had to use sign language to each other, even when Paul and George were singing into the same microphone, but, far from being discouraged, they played and sang marvellously. I had great difficulty getting near the stage until a friendly policeman realized my predicament and escorted me to a more favourable vantage point.

Washington, 12 February 1964
(104) On our return to Union Station from the Shoreham Hotel, I spotted the famous Capitol Building and asked our driver to stop the car for a few minutes. I persuaded John to pose with the famous cupola behind him. It was a snowy day, crisp and cold.

Miami, February 1964
(105) Preparing for rehearsals at the Napoleon Rooms in Miami's Deauville Hotel, where the second *Ed Sullivan Show* was due to be televised. **(106)** John warming up, during the actual performance, for the first number. **(107)** John in particular had been impressed by Cassius Clay, especially after being snubbed early by the current champ, Sonny Liston, who didn't want to pose with the boys. Fight promoter Harold Conrad invited them to the gym to watch Clay work out; they all went haywire and jumped at the chance. The Beatles didn't mind Clay showing off at their expense, but they were just as quick with their cheeky retorts as the soon-to-be champ (soon to be renamed Muhammad Ali). **(108, 109)** John and Cynthia at the poolside of a villa owned by local millionaire Bernie Castro, where they were able to spend their free time in relative privacy. **(110)** This is the picture of mine which so upset John when it was published in *Tit Bits* a few weeks later. I like the picture but when I look at it now I know why he was annoyed. It caused a rift between John and myself that lasted several years. **(111)** The boys were mesmerized by a flash umbrella being used in bright sunlight for photographer John Loengard's famous front-cover colour photograph for *Life* magazine. Loengard had a whole staff with him, including photographic assistants and an electrician. And all for one picture . . . **(112)** Perhaps the fact that John was so easily distracted from his fishing contributed to the fact that he caught absolutely nothing. George was easily the fishing champ on this trip. **(113)** Playing hide-and-seek with Cynthia in the corner of the pool at Bernie Castro's villa. **(114)** This beautifully-made English peak cap with a 'Beatles' emblem was one of the few pieces of merchandise that the boys' wouldn't endorse; the reason, I discovered, was that it hid their hair. **(115)** At the home of Sgt. Buddy Dresner, the officer assigned by the Miami Police Department to protect the Beatles. I don't think Sgt. Dresner was the prototype for Sgt. Pepper – here he is introducing John to the sweet taste of bourbon. **(116)** The children of the house crowd around John by the pool. The flight bag in the picture, with the cleverly adapted Beatles logo, was a souvenir from Paris.

New York, arrival from Miami, 20 February 1964
(117) Return to the frozen north and New York newsmen.

Return to Heathrow, 22 February 1964
(118) A wide-angle shot of the Beatles' return to a tumultuous welcome at London's Heathrow Airport. A similar picture of mine was used on the centre-spread of next day's *Daily Mirror*, but the sheer number of people there caused a furore with the airport authorities because it was against regulations for so many newsmen to be on the tarmac. They held an enquiry after the incident and requested some of my pictures as evidence. I felt quite guilty because there were some sackings as a result.

EMI Studios, 25 February 1964
At the first recording session after the American triumph, the boys recorded the vocals on 'Can't Buy Me Love' and 'You Can't Do That', and versions of 'Long Tall Sally', 'Matchbox', 'I Call Your Name', and 'Slowdown'. It was also George's 21st birthday. **(119, 120, 121)** John in no. 2 studio, recording and between takes. **(122, 123, 124, 125, 126)** He listens animatedly to the playbacks. **(127, 128)** The Beatles team, with George Martin and engineer Norman 'Hurricane' Smith, at work during remixing.

***A Hard Day's Night*, March and April 1964**
(129, 130) The complete set for the TV pop show *Ready Steady Go* was reconstructed at Twickenham for a section in their first film. **(131)** Their BBC stomping ground, the Paris Cinema, was also used in the movie; here's John eyeball-to-eyeball with veteran Scots actor John Laurie. **(132)** John isn't praying but merely resting his eyes. He was short-sighted and the strong film lights quickly strained them. **(133)** John autographs a photograph for a lucky Swedish schoolgirl who won a prize to visit the Beatles on set for a day. Looking on is a Swedish journalist covering the story and acting as interpreter.

***Around the Beatles*, 27 April 1964**
(134) The Jack Good-produced ATV spectacular cast the fab four in a revolutionary interpretation of Shakespeare's *A Midsummer Night's Dream*. Here's John, as pretty a Thisbe as was ever portrayed. Did ye Bard twist in his grave?

EMI House, London, June 1964
(135) One of a series of portraits I took of all four boys at Manchester Square.

NEMS offices, London, June 1964
(136) This was an impromptu shot taken during an interview at NEMS' new offices in Argyll Street. The hand lighting John's cigarette belongs to George.

***Top Gear*, 16 July 1964**
(137) BBC radio's *Top Gear* went out on Thursdays between 10.00 pm and midnight. Presented by Brian Matthew and produced by Bernie Andrews, it was the BBC's first 'progressive' music show and this shot was taken on the Beatles' first *Top Gear* performance. They featured seven songs on the show and here is John singing 'I Should Have Known Better'.

***Night of a Thousand Stars*, 23 July 1964**
(138) At a charity show held at the London Palladium, John meets another great Englishman, Sir Laurence Olivier, who, John must have hoped, hadn't seen him as Thisbe two months earlier.

Blackpool, 26 July 1964
(139,140) First-thing-in-the-morning John after the Beatles' show at the Opera House in Blackpool. In one picture he looks like Bob Dylan, whose influence John was just beginning to reflect. In the other shot John mistakes a cup of tea for the telephone.

Heathrow Airport, London, August 1964
(141) John and Cynthia at London's Heathrow Airport, about to depart for their second North American trip.

Elstree Studios, November 1964
(142) Rehearsals at Elstree film studios for ATV's *Thank Your Lucky Stars*.

Hammersmith Odeon, London, December 1964
(143, 144) The Beatles' Christmas Show ran for three weeks and made a pleasant change because there were actually some boys in the audience. Most of Epstein's NEMS artists took part, with Rolf Harris again compering.

EMI Studios, February 1965
(145) John catches some winter sunshine in the lovely, well-kept garden at the back of St John's Wood studio while he was taking a break from the recording of songs for the Beatles' second film *Help*.

Saville Theatre, London, 26 October 1965
(146) 'Now you see it, now you don't . . .' John swinging his 'gong' at the MBE press conference held onstage at Brian Epstein's newly-acquired Saville Theatre in Shaftesbury Avenue.

Twickenham Studios, March 1965
(147) I wandered on to the *Help* set and encountered an improvised white background – a sheet – and director Dick Lester in deep discussion with John, who was nearly ready for the take.

Richmond Jazz Festival, August 1965
(148) Coming out of the car park into the festival, John is waylaid by a fan; he obliges her with a smile and a signature.

Madame Tussaud's, London, May 1967
(149) The remarkable effigy **(150)** of John Lennon, MBE, as unveiled at London's famous waxworks. It has since been replaced by a model of John from his earlier mop-top period, for which the waxworks used my photographs to obtain the likeness.

***Sergeant Pepper* press reception, London, May 1967**
(151, 152) The press were invited to Brian Epstein's Belgravia home to hear the latest (and most famous) Beatles album, while there was a photo call at Apple offices in Savile Row. John was very forthcoming about the BBC ban on 'A Day in the Life'; 'It's nothing to do with drugs, they've got it all wrong,' he stated. But ban or no ban, John was exceptionally good-humoured that day. Artistically, it was probably the Beatles' finest hour.

EMI Studios, 25 June 1967
(154) 'All You Need Is Love' was recorded as part of the first live world-wide TV programme *Our World* as seen, so it was said, in 24 countries by over 400 million people. **(153)** All the boys became sandwich-board men, holding up flower-power boards with words from the song's title. John gets the verb. **(155)** Up, up and away . . . in the background behind John is Tony Barrow, who started at NEMS by running their official fan club and soon went on to become their press officer. **(156)** Although the backing on 'All You Need Is Love' had been pre-recorded, John did add the lead vocal on the show itself. And he shaved off his moustache for the occasion.

***Dee Time*, London, February 1970**
(157) Taken around the time the Beatles were breaking up, this shot shows a radical-looking John appearing on Simon Dee's chat show. **(158)** Left to right, Michael X, Yoko, John and Simon Dee. John came on the show, encouraged by Yoko, in order to publicize Michael X, the self-proclaimed British black power leader. **(159)** The new profile. **(160)** With Yoko.